PAGES, PICTURES, AND PRINT

Pages, Pictures, and Print

A BOOK IN THE MAKING

WRITTEN AND ILLUSTRATED

BY JOANNA FOSTER

NEW YORK

HARCOURT, BRACE & WORLD, INC.

This book is gratefully dedicated to all the many people whose encouragement and assistance brought it into being. Most especially it is dedicated to GF.

I am also indebted to my many friends at Harcourt, Brace & World for putting up with an author in their midst, and to the following for their very helpful readings of the manuscript: Mr. William Gleason of Colonial Press, Inc.; Mr. Gerald Konecky of Graphic Offset Corp.; Mr. Franklin A. Sears of Connecticut Printers, Inc., Kellogg and Bulkeley Division; Mr. Kenneth James of Publishers Book Bindery, Inc.; Mr. Milton Shapiro of Collier Photo Engraving Company, Inc.; Miss Katherine Love of the New York Public Library; and Mr. Daniel Melcher of R. R. Bowker Company.

Among many other companies who helped me in gathering information, I would like to thank especially the Smyth Manufacturing Company; Quinn and Boden Company, Inc.; John F. Cuneo Company; Lithographic Technical Foundation; Rainbow Plate Company; H. Wolff Book Manufacturing Company, Inc.; Miehle Printing Press and Manufacturing Company; American Type Founders Company, Inc.; and the Mergenthaler Linotype Company. I would also like to express my appreciation to the American Institute of Graphic Arts Workshop for the opportunity to work with type and printing and to *The Making of Books* by Séan Jennett, which was a source of unfailing refreshment and inspiration.

Contents

1 / A Story and a Manuscript

A book slides across the library desk. "That's the best book I've ever read. Is there another by the same author?"

"I'm afraid not," answers the librarian. "The author's writing a new one, but it won't be published until the fall."

"What makes it take so long?"

This is the story of what takes so long, of all the things that must happen to a book before it gets to the reader. Scores of people have a part in this story, but it all begins with one person, the author. Let's suppose, in this case, that you are the author. You have decided to write a book, and this is what might happen.

Before you put down any words, you must have something to say. Through your book you will be talking to hundreds and thousands of people you have never met. What do you have to tell that they will find interesting?

Perhaps you have made up some fairy tales. Before you decide on one of these for your book, look in the library. You will find that there are already hundreds of good fairy tales for people to read. It would be better to write a story that is more especially yours, one that no one else can tell as well. Think about the things you've done and the people that you know.

Let's suppose that you have a brother who is good at inventing all kinds of wonderful devices. These inventions in themselves wouldn't make a story, but people are always saying about him, "What will that boy dream up next!" This is where you let your imagination take over. What might your brother dream up next? What surprising results would his new invention lead to? In the answer to these questions you find the plot for a story.

If the incidents for this story begin popping into your head, now is the time to start putting words on paper. Sentence by sentence, page by page — the words come slowly at first. But as you keep on, they come faster and faster, and at times it almost seems as if the characters have taken over and are telling the story themselves.

As long as things are going this well, you push on with the story. But at some point you will probably bog down. To get started again, you go over what you have done, revising and rewriting it. Some authors write one chapter at a time and then rewrite that until they have it just the way they want it. Others write a whole section of the book before they read and revise it.

Many authors will not even begin as you did. Some think about their book for years before they start to write. Some outline their story and make many notes first. Often authors have to do research and collect a great deal of information before they begin. Much of this research can be done by reading books, but some involves traveling and talking to experts on a subject. Another kind of research is done by experimenting. The author of a science or a how-to-do-it book, for example, wants to make sure that none of his instructions will cause an unexpected explosion!

It may take weeks or months to get all the words on paper. One day, however, the first copy, or draft, of your story is finished. It sounds fine and you go to bed delighted with your accomplish-

ment. The next morning your pleasure fades. It doesn't read nearly as well as you had thought. It is wordy in some spots; hazy in others, and there is much that could be improved. Back to work. By rewriting here, cutting there, shifting paragraphs somewhere else, you bring a revised or second draft into being. There may be a third and even a fourth draft before you are satisfied. Some authors have rewritten a single sentence more than a hundred times before it pleased them. Writing is an enjoyable but not a particularly easy job!

Finally the story is the way you want it. The precious pile of typewritten pages you have in front of you is at last a finished manuscript. The word "manuscript" is the proper name for your story at this stage. Only after your story is printed and bound will it actually be a book.

Changing manuscripts into books and selling these books to stores and libraries is the job of the publisher. Generally, a publisher is not just one person but a company, called a publishing house, made up of many people. There are some twenty-four big publishing houses in the United States, and well over two hundred smaller ones. In a directory called *The Literary Market Place* you will find listed about ninety-six of these that publish books for children. This is the kind of book you have written, so you have a wide choice.

You begin your search for a publisher by mail, since they must have time to read your story before saying whether or not they'll publish it. As you take your manuscript to the post office, you wonder how long it will be before you get an answer — a week or maybe two? It seems hard to wait even that long. But strengthen your patience, for it may take as long as five or six weeks.

Several days after you handed your manuscript through the window at the post office, it arrives in the mail room of the publishing house, along with several others.

"These are juveniles," calls the clerk to the office boy. "Will you take them down to trade when you go." Thus, your manuscript and the others are delivered to the office of the editor of children's books. This office is in the trade division, the part of the publishing house that publishes the books you find in bookstores and libraries. This particular publishing house also has a textbook division, which publishes the books written especially for use in schools. Not all publishing houses will be divided in this way. Some may have only one of these divisions.

Your manuscript has reached the right office, but it is hardly alone! After its arrival has been noted on a card, it goes to the bottom of a tall stack of manuscripts in the office safe. This awesome pile consists of the four or five manuscripts that arrived yesterday, which, in turn, are under the twenty-five or thirty that came in the week before. Big ones, small ones, fat ones, skinny ones — the manuscripts are every shape and size and come from all over the United States. Some, such as yours, have come in directly from the author. Others in the pile were first sent to literary agents who in turn submit them to the various publishers.

In due time your manuscript gets to the top of the pile and is in line for its first reading. One of the editor's assistants slips it from the envelope, writes the title on a report sheet, and leans back in her chair ready to read. Now your story is on its own.

As she reads, she begins to smile, enjoying some of the amusing incidents. At the same time she is thinking about the story as a whole. Do these incidents fit together into a well-built story? Do the boy, his family, and friends come alive? Would they really do the things described? Does the story make you want to keep reading right up to the end?

Before she begins her report, she also thinks about your story in relation to the three hundred or so other children's books this publishing house has on its list to sell. Is your story different from these? Is it outstanding enough to merit a place among the twenty-five or thirty children's books that will be added to the list next year? There is keen competition for these twenty-five or thirty places! Each year about a thousand manuscripts by new authors come in as well as many manuscripts by authors whose earlier books have been published by this house.

If your story is really good and deserves to be published, it probably will be — if not by this publisher, then by another. There are many more publishing houses to try, should you get a rejection slip from this one.

At the bottom of her report on your manuscript the assistant writes, "This has possibilities. I recommend a second reading." By the end of that day your manuscript is on the editor's desk.

Probably not the next day or the day after, but before too long, the editor will close her door, push aside the hundred-and-one things that are demanding attention, and pick up your manuscript. One of the special pleasures of being an editor is finding a new author and a new story worth publishing. She picks up your manuscript hopefully.

"There is freshness and originality about that story," she says later, talking with her assistant. "Here and there the construction is weak, but the writing has spark and the characterization is good on the whole. Only the parents seem wooden and rather goody-goody, but I think we could work this out with the author. There is certainly a demand for good humorous stories like this." The following day the editor writes you a letter.

The six long weeks you've waited are quickly forgotten when the letter arrives. In it the editor writes that she likes the manuscript but has some improvements to suggest. If these changes seem possible to you, she would like to publish your story. It doesn't take long to write back that, yes, you're willing to try!

Some of the improvements can be done quickly. Others, such as making the parents seem more true to life, are harder to work out. Your editor's letter suggested some of the ways it might be done and those suggestions lead you to think of still others. Your own mother certainly isn't always as patient with your brother's inventions as the mother in your story. And the father might be like yours in always wanting to read aloud from his newspaper at dinner. But you can't put in too much more about the mother and father or it will stop the action of the story.

This revision is like working a crossword puzzle except that now, luckily, you have someone to help you. Between you and the editor, letters fly back and forth for another three or four weeks. Finally the manuscript is in its finished form. The story

is now as good as the two of you can make it.

In her next letter, the editor writes about the contract, which is a legal agreement that both you and the publisher will sign. The contract states that the publisher will manufacture and sell your book and will pay you what is known as a royalty on every copy that is sold. The amount of the royalty on your book might be twenty to twenty-five cents a copy.

Your contract will also cover many other details. Among these is the way in which the money will be divided between you and the publisher if your book is made into a movie, or published later in another country, or used on radio or television. At the bottom of the last page will be the signature of the president or another official of the publishing house. Beside it will be a line for your signature.

Instead of mailing your finished manuscript and the signed contract to the editor, you may be able to deliver it to her in person. Be sure also to take a corrected carbon copy of your manuscript with you.

President

Conference Room

Design and Production Department

Children's Book Department

Copy Editor

Adult Book Editors

Advertising, Promotion and Publicity Department

Permissions Department

Sales Department

2 / From Editor to Designer

The offices of your publisher, which take up two floors of a large office building, are in New York City, where many — though certainly not all — publishing houses are located. If, as you zoom up in the elevator, you are expecting to see books actually being put together, you will probably be disappointed. The offices of a publishing house look and sound very much like those of any other business except that there are more books around.

An appealing display of new books greets you as you enter the reception room. But before there is really a chance to look at them, you are whisked back to your editor's office. Here are more books, shelves and shelves of them. There is even a pile of books on her desk. This pile is mostly new children's books from other publishers. It is important for your editor to keep up with the new books that are being published elsewhere for children.

Looking around, you see on the walls above the bookcase several picture-book illustrations that have been framed and also the brightly colored poster for Children's Book Week. The yearly celebration of Book Week is sponsored by the Children's Book Council, a nonprofit organization to which your publisher and the others who do children's books belong.

On the editor's desk, along with magazines, papers, and folders of letters, you will probably see four or five fat manila envelopes. These are several of the other manuscripts your editor is working on. Besides yours, she is preparing at least fourteen others for publication next season. Propped up nearby are the illustrations for one of these. The artist has just been in to discuss them with the editor.

While you are here, the editor talks to you about choosing an artist for your book. The illustrations will be black-and-white line drawings, she explains, and there will be room for fourteen pages of them. That means that your book may have as many as twenty-one pictures, since some will be only a half or a third of a page in size.

"Here are some drawings by an artist we can always count on for a good job. He has a quick, free style and could, I think, catch the spirit of your story. Shall we try him?" the editor asks.

This artist seems a fine choice to you, so your editor makes a note to call and have him come in to see her within the next few days. She will discuss the book and its pictures with him, the fee the publisher will pay him, and then give him the carbon copy of your manuscript to read. While the original copy of your manuscript is going through its next steps, the artist will be working on the illustrations.

As this is your first visit to a publishing house, your editor may next take you on a tour of the offices and introduce you to some of the other people who will be working with your book.

Across from your editor's office is the office of the copy editor. She is the person to whom your manuscript will go next. Commas, capitals, misspelled words — these and all other points of grammar, punctuation, and spelling are checked by the copy editor. She will also be keeping an eagle eye out for anything in your story that may be inconsistent or confusing. Though the editor will catch many of these things, every so often something slips through unnoticed. It is particularly important for the copy editor to catch such slips in informational or historical books, but for any manuscript this final checking and polishing is wise.

Down the aisle, past the editors of adult books, is the office of the man who handles contracts and permissions. He is explaining over the phone that, in order to use any part of a book in a magazine or other publication, written permission must be given by your publisher. This is the man who will be looking out for the rights of your book as they are stated in the contract.

Across the way is the department that does advertising, promotion, and publicity. As the manager rises to shake your hand, you see that he has been going over several ads for the new adult books. In an adjoining office is a girl with pages and pages of a catalog spread out before her. She is checking and correcting these in preparation for a new printing. Posters, circulars, and author appearances on radio and television are all part of the work of people in this department. They will be responsible for spreading the news of your book.

On down the aisle is the sales department. You can spot it by the order forms on the desks. Most of these orders are from bookstores and libraries. But there are also several large orders from the wholesale companies that buy from many publishers and fill the orders of the libraries and stores that the publisher's salesmen cannot visit. The books to fill these orders are not kept in this building. They are stored in a warehouse and will be shipped from there. You will have a chance to meet the sales manager, but not the other eight salesmen. They are now out on selling trips all over the United States.

Through a door are the accounting and billing departments. In there, along with the regular sound of typewriters and telephones, you will hear the beat of the rapid adding machines.

Here are the people who will pay the bills for the making of your book. They will also collect the money for the copies that are sold and every six months send you a royalty check.

At the other end of the floor are the president's office and the conference room. And next to them is the design and production department. Upstairs are the offices of the textbook division.

The design and production department is the only place in the publishing house where you are sure to catch a glimpse of books as they look before they are finished. Looking around, you will see bundles of long pieces of paper stored on shelves and in cabinets, tall rolls of paper leaning in a corner, a pile of sample book covers back of one of the desks, and several unbound books on one of the tables.

Near the windows are the drawing boards used by the designers. Sometimes a designer will also handle the production, or manufacturing, of a book. In the case of your book, however, the production man on the phone over there is going to do it. He has, in fact, already done a good deal of work on your book.

Before the editor could send you a contract offering a certain royalty, she first had to know how much it would cost to make the book and at what price it would have to be sold. To give her this information, the production man made up an estimate of all the expenses. These include the cost of the materials, such as paper and cloth, and the heavy costs of printing and binding the book. Most publishers do not print and bind their own books. Instead, they hire other specialized companies to do this. It is the production man who will make all these arrangements and see that everything runs smoothly.

As soon as he knows the size of your book and the number of copies that are to be printed, the production man will order the paper for it. While you are talking with him, he may show you various samples of book paper. "Your book will be printed by

letterpress and have line drawings, so we will probably use a paper like this one." The sample he hands you is a pale cream color. Though its surface is even, it is not a smooth, glossy paper as are some of the other samples.

"The surface on the one in your hand is called an Antique finish. Another kind of book and another method of printing would call for a different finish. Besides different kinds and qualities of book paper, there is also a great variety of color and thickness from which to choose."

These samples are the size of book pages, but this is not the way the paper will be delivered to the printer. Sometimes it is shipped from the paper mills in great rolls. More often it comes as a stack of large sheets packed on a wooden platform called a skid. The production man has several of these large sheets of paper standing rolled up behind his desk. Spreading one out, he shows you how big it is. This one happens to be 44 by 66 inches. The size that he will order for your book will depend on the number of pages in it, their shape, and how they are to be bound.

What will the shape of yours be, and what is it actually going to look like? The person who can tell you is the designer. He will draw up the final plans for it when he receives your manuscript from the copy editor. He has, however, already talked with the editor about your book.

Since it is a book for older children, it does not need a special shape such as a picture book or a book for younger readers. The designer has a sample book with blank pages in it that is exactly the shape that your book is going to be. If you want to know the size, borrow the long metal ruler on his drawing board. The page measures 5⅝ inches wide by 8 inches high.

Those are the figures, provided you used the side of the ruler marked off in inches. If, however, you use the other side of the ruler, you would get 32 by 48. Quite a difference!

"These are picas you're measuring now, not inches," explains the designer. "We figure six picas to an inch, and each pica is divided into twelve smaller parts called points. It's a special kind of measurement used in printing — not so important for measuring the book itself, but very important for measuring type."

In almost all that he does, the designer is working with type. Type is the name given to all printed letters, and the many different styles these letters come in are called type faces. On a shelf near the designer are several fat books with page after page of alphabets and sample paragraphs in the different type faces. You might have trouble telling one face from another, but the designer can spot the difference for you right away. Just as you can recognize a friend's handwriting, he can tell a type face by the shape of its letters.

"One thing to look for is the shape of the serifs. Those are the tiny cross marks that finish off each stroke in a letter. Some faces have thin flat ones, Caledonia for example, while others are rounded such as those on the Caslon letters. Futura, on the other hand, is one of the sans-serif faces with no serifs at all."

ABCDEFGHIJKLMNOPQRSTUVWXYZ
abcdefghijklmnopqrstuvwxyz   1234567890
[ ] % † § ‡ ¶ * ( ) $,.-;':'!? & ⅛ ¼ ⅜ ⅝ ¾ ⅞

This is an alphabet and punctuation marks of 11-point Janson. These lines are leaded three points.

𝕲𝖚𝖙𝖊𝖓𝖇𝖊𝖗𝖌 𝖚𝖘𝖊𝖉 𝖆 𝖇𝖑𝖆𝖈𝖐 𝖑𝖊𝖙𝖙𝖊𝖗 𝖙𝖞𝖕𝖊 𝖒𝖚𝖈𝖍 𝖑𝖎𝖐𝖊 𝖙𝖍𝖎𝖘 𝖋𝖆𝖈𝖊 𝖜𝖍𝖎𝖈𝖍 𝖎𝖘 𝖈𝖆𝖑𝖑𝖊𝖉 𝕺𝖑𝖉 𝕰𝖓𝖌𝖑𝖎𝖘𝖍.

The face Cloister was inspired by the beautiful roman letters designed in 1470 by a Venetian named Jenson.

Another Italian printer of that time, Aldus Manutius, created the slanted italic letter forms. This is the italic of a face called Old Style.

This face is named for Garamond, a French type designer who lived in the early 1500's.

Caslon, an Englishman, designed this type face when George Washington was a boy.

The face Baskerville is one with rounded serifs and is called an old style face.

Caledonia has flat serifs and is called a modern face. (It is the one used in this book.)

Bodoni is a face with many relatives: a bold one, a condensed one, an open one.

Sans-serif faces like this one, Futura, became especially popular after 1925.

Electra is the design of W. A. Dwiggins, one of the outstanding American type designers of the past fifty years.

Most type faces come in several sizes, which are measured in points. The size is measured as the number of points between the top of a tall letter like "l" and the bottom of a long letter like "p." Each face also is likely to have both regular, or roman, letters and the slanted, or italic, letters. Italics are used for such things as book and magazine titles, foreign words, or a certain word that the author wants to emphasize.

As you go through the designer's type book, you will see that the faces vary in feeling. One seems particularly graceful, another crisp and businesslike, one delicate, another bold and forthright. Although new type faces are still being made up, some of the ones you see most often are taken from designs hundreds of years old. Many of these — such as Garamond, Bodoni, Caslon, and Baskerville — are named after famous men in the history of printing.

Another thing that you will notice is that some of the sample pages seem easier to read than others. This is not always because of the type size. It can be the shape of the letters. Or it can be the amount of space left between the lines of type. This space is called "leading," and the designer indicates the amount he wants in points.

For your book, the designer selects 11-point Janson type with three points of leading between each line. This type face was inspired by the designs of Anton Janson, a Dutchman who lived in Leipzig around the year 1670. It has a sturdy, compact feeling and yet is easy to read. It is appropriate to your story and will also go well with the kind of illustrations that the book will have. This type will be used all through your book except for the chapter titles and the first few pages before the actual story starts.

When your manuscript comes to the designer, he first must determine exactly how long it is. A letter is also called a character, and the designer's assistant does what is called a character count to find the total number of letters, or characters, in the manuscript. To do this, he counts the total number of lines and multiplies that figure by the average number of characters in a line.

The designer now draws a master plan, showing exactly how a page is to look — how wide the lines of type are to be, what each margin should measure, the number of lines to a page, and where the page number is to go. It also shows the placement of the running head, which is the book or chapter title that, in your book will appear at the top of each page. Having settled on this master plan, the designer can now calculate that your book will have 168 pages of story, 14 pages of illustration, and 10 pages of introductory or front matter. Your book will have 192 pages in all.

The front matter, which the designer will plan later, comprises the pages that come before the story begins. The first of

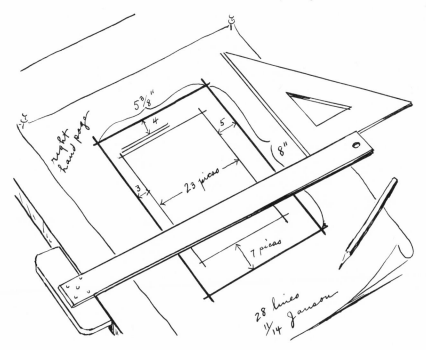

these pages is the half title. This simply gives the title of your book and acts as an usher, sending the reader on to the title page. Here is the formal introduction to your book, giving all the important information: the full title, your name, the artist's name, the publisher, the city where it was published, and sometimes the year of publication. If the year doesn't appear here, it will always be found on the next page. This is the copyright page. It has a short paragraph that says no one may copy anything out of your book for publication without permission. A dedication page may follow, then the table of contents, and finally another half-title, this time ushering the reader into the story proper. The front matter in books varies. This is the pattern for yours. Other books may have more pages of front matter, and some will have fewer. They may also have back matter, pages that come after the story, such as an index or a bibliography, which your book does not have.

About three weeks after your visit to the publishing house, your manuscript has been copy edited and designed. Now it is ready for the typesetter. Down to the production man's desk goes the manuscript. A phone call is made to the printer, and the manuscript is on its way by messenger. With it go the designer's plans and a sheet of instructions. When your manuscript returns to the publishing house, it will have been set in type.

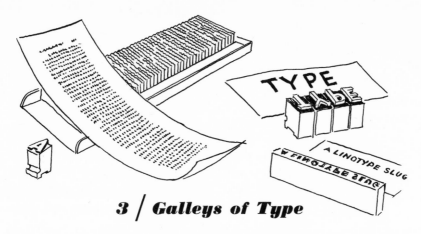

3 / Galleys of Type

A journey across town and your manuscript arrives at the printer's office, a busy place, alive with the sound of typewriters and telephones. Forty or more different books are being worked on in this printing plant, and the progress of each one must be kept track of in this office. From here your manuscript goes to the foreman of the composing room, who will be in charge of it for the next few weeks. He will have it set in type by his men, who are called compositors or typesetters.

To hear the foreman over the noise of the composing room takes some close listening. "We'll be setting all of your book on one of those Linotype machines over there with the exception of the chapter headings and some of the front matter. The type for those will be set by hand." The Linotype machines, which are making most of the noise in the room, are just one of several kinds of machines that set type. Another, called Monotype, is also used for books, but usually for books that are more complicated than yours. There are also several methods of setting type photographically, called photosetting, but that would probably not be done here.

You will, however, see compositors setting type by hand. Hand-setting is done much as it was five hundred years ago when printing began. Printing as we know it today began with the famous

Gutenberg Bible, which was completed in the year 1455, just thirty-seven years before Columbus discovered America. Until that time every copy of every book had been written out by hand. Each copy of a book took a great deal of time to make and so was very expensive. Books were treasures that only the wealthy could afford to own and read.

As more and more people learned to read, more and cheaper books were needed. Many men experimented with ways to copy books faster. Printing seemed to be the answer. At first, they carved the words and pictures for a page on a wooden block. Because the words and pictures stood up from the block, they could be easily inked. A piece of paper was put on the block and pressed so that the ink came off on it. As this piece was lifted off, the block was inked again and another piece of paper was put on it, and then another and another. But for each page a separate block had to be carved, and once enough copies of that page had been printed the block was useless. Making the blocks was a slow and exacting process, and printing in this way proved impractical.

Johann Gutenberg knew of this kind of printing and perhaps also of the attempts at printing with each letter carved on a separate small wooden block. Being a goldsmith, he also knew the ways of working and molding metals. For years he worked on the problems of type and printing and finally came up with this solution. For each letter of the alphabet, he made a mold. He connected this to another small, boxlike mold. This second one would give the letter a base to stand on. Into this combined mold, he poured hot metal, a combination of lead, tin, and antimony. When the metal had cooled and hardened, he lifted it out — a small neatly shaped piece with a raised letter on one end. Closing the mold again, he poured more metal into it and made a duplicate of the first piece. Taking each letter in turn, he made many exact copies of it. These individual pieces of metal became known as pieces of type.

Spelling out the words and sentences of a manuscript, Gutenberg soon had a page of lines in type. These were fastened together firmly and then printed as if they were a single block. However, that was not the end of the type pieces. Once he had printed enough copies of that page, the pieces of type could be rearranged into new words and sentences and another page could be made.

To keep the many pieces of type in usable order, they were sorted into a large flat tray that was divided into sections. Each section held the pieces for one particular letter. Such a tray is still used for hand-setting and is called a case. Though modern cases are arranged differently, they look much like the ones used in Gutenberg's time.

Where men are setting type by hand, you will see that the cabinets in front of them have wide thin drawers. These are the cases of type. Each case holds the alphabet and punctuation marks for just one size of one type face. Once it was common to have two cases for each size. One held the small letters of the face and the other the capital letters. When these two cases were put on the slanted top of the cabinet, the one holding the capital letters was put above the other. The capitals, therefore, began to be called upper case letters, and the small letters, lower case. People who work with books and printing still refer to letters as being either lower case or upper case, rather than small letters and capitals.

Little hand-setting is done today because it is so much slower than by machine. But it is still useful when only a small amount of a special type face or size is needed. In your manuscript, for instance, the chapter headings and some of the front matter will be set by hand. This is how it is done.

To begin with, the compositor pulls out a case of 18-point Lydian, which is the type face that the designer specified for your chapter headings. Placing the case on the slanted counter, he takes a special metal holder in his left hand and adjusts it to the length of line he wants. This holder is called a stick, and into it go the pieces of type that he picks rapidly one by one from the case. As he goes along, he puts in punctuation marks and also blank pieces of type metal to make the spaces between the words.

Almost everyone in the composing room is a master at reading letters upside down. They do it almost as fast as you can read right side up. The reason for this is that they set type with the letters upside down. If this sounds odd, look at a piece of type and perhaps you can figure out why this is the best way to do it. You will see that the letter on a piece of type faces backward. It is reversed like this so that when it is inked and turned over onto paper, the printed letter will come out facing in the right direction. If the compositor set these backward letters right side up, he would have to work not only from right to left but probably from the bottom of a page to the top. By working with the letters upside down, he can move from left to right and also do the lines in their normal order.

Most of the type for your book will be set by the Linotype operator. The Linotype machine in front of which he sits looks very complicated, but in some ways it is similar to hand-setting. Just as the hand compositor must select the proper case from which to work, the Linotype operator must select what is called a magazine. This is a large flat box. On the machine you will see it fastened so that it slants down from the top. Like the case, the magazine usually holds only one size of one type face. However, instead of holding actual pieces of type, as the case does, the magazine holds molds for each of the different letters. These are called matrices.

Moving his fingers over the blue, white, and black keys, the operator selects the matrices as if he were typing. But the keys on the Linotype machine are far more sensitive than those on an ordinary typewriter. He barely has to touch a key to have a matrix slip out of the magazine down into the stick. The stick on the Linotype machine is called the assembler. Like a hand stick it can be adjusted for lines of different lengths.

Twenty-three picas — that is the length specified on the designer's plan for your book. The operator sets his assembler for this, props the first pages of your manuscript above the keyboard, and begins. As his fingers brush over the keys, the matrices for the first words come clinking down into the assembler. Between each word, he touches the space bar, and an adjustable spaceband drops into the line. These spacebands are the means by which the machine can make all of the lines the same length. If a line runs a little short of the twenty-three pica width, the spacebands will automatically expand each of the spaces between the words to fill out the line.

When the assembler is filled, the operator presses a lever that shifts this line of matrices to the casting part of the machine. From this point on, all the operations are automatic. The second part of the Linotype machine looks something like a sidecar to the first. This is where the casting is done. With a clanking sound the line of matrices moves in front of a slit that opens from a bubbling pot of hot type metal. A plunger is pushed into the pot and a strong squirt of hot metal rushes through the slit into the matrices. Thus the letters are molded. The shape of the opening for the hot lead is such that the line will come out standing on one long base of metal.

There is more clanking, as knives trim the sides of this newly molded line of type, ingloriously called a slug. Cooled and hardened, the metal slug drops from the molds and comes sliding down onto a narrow tray. A metal arm picks up the line of empty matrices and lifts them to the top of the magazine where they go traveling along a distributor bar. This bar is designed so that it drops each matrix back into its proper place in the magazine where it is ready to be used again.

While all of this is happening, the operator is preparing another line of matrices that is now ready to be cast. After that second slug comes sliding down into the tray, there will be another and then another. The words of your manuscript are turned into type at the rate of about four lines, or slugs, a minute.

Gutenberg first cast his type and then assembled it, as did all the printers who followed him. In time, special companies called type foundries took over casting the type for printers. Such companies still produce the pieces of type that are used in hand-setting.

The Linotype machine, developed in the United States by Ottmar Mergenthaler and first used in the year 1886, does both steps but reverses them. It first assembles the letters in the form of matrices or molds and *then* casts the type from them. The letters are not cast separately, as Gutenberg did it, but are cast as a group to form a solid slug or line of type, which is where the machine gets its name.

The metal that is used, like that of the early printers, is a mixture of lead, tin, and antimony, and the slugs that drop into the tray have a shiny silver color. As soon as a number of lines are finished, they are taken off onto another tray. These long narrow trays are called galleys. Everywhere you look in the composing room, you will see them. There are galleys on the small proving presses. There are galleys being worked over at the large tables in the middle of the room. And there are many more stored in the racks below the tables and against the walls.

The galleys for each book are stored in a special section of these shelves. But before the apprentice puts them away, he will run a trial printing of them on the proving press. All trial printings are called proofs. Because these first proofs are printed from the slugs while they are in the galleys, they are called galley proofs. A galley holds enough lines for about three pages of your book, so the galley proofs are printed on long sheets of paper. With this first printing, the slugs have begun their working life. No longer are they silvery, for the black printing ink has left them gray.

You have to shout to be heard over the noise in the composing room, so it is startling to follow the freshly printed galley proofs into a hushed room where you barely hear the drone of low voices. This is where the proofreaders work. It is their job to see that the galleys are exactly like the manuscript. A word may be misspelled, a letter may be upside down or fuzzy, a comma may have been left out, or too much space may have been put in. The proofreader is on the lookout for these and any other errors.

When such a mistake is spotted, it is marked according to a code of proofreader's marks. These marks tell the typesetter exactly what is wrong and how to correct it. This saves long and sometimes confusing explanations, so not only proofreaders, but also designers, editors, and experienced authors like to use this code when they are working with manuscripts and proofs.

ℒ	This mark means take out
∧	This means put in here
stet	Disregard the change— let it stay as it is
#	Put in space
⌣	Take out some space
◯	Close up completely
¶	Start a new paragraph
⊓	Move up
⊔	Move down
℧	Turn over
⸠	Move to the left
⸡	Move to the right

ital	Change to italics
rom	Change to roman letters
l.c.	Change to lower case letters
Caps	Change to capital letters
⊙	Put in a period
⋀	Put in a comma
⋁	Put in an apostrophe
⋁	Put in a quotation mark
⸗	Put in a hyphen
?	Asking the author, "Is this right?"

The Linotype operator resets the lines that need correcting, and the proofreader checks the galley proofs once more. Then they are bundled up and sent back to the publishing house with the manuscript. There are usually several sets of these galley proofs. One set will be for you. One goes to the designer, and one will stay on file in the production department. The master set will be held by the copy editor. It will be the one to go back to the printer with any changes that you or your editor want to make.

Prepare yourself for a strange and very pleasant experience the day that your galley proofs arrive in the mail. Here is your story. No longer is it just so many dog-eared pages of typewriting as when you last saw it about a month and a half ago. Now it lies before you, a packet of long narrow sheets with even, orderly lines of black type. Strangely enough, as you begin to read, it sounds much better than you remembered it. What a pleasure to be able to read your story almost as if someone else had written it! But eventually you'll hit a rough spot that you will want to improve. Sometimes important changes are needed — things that neither you nor your editor were aware of earlier. This is why your publisher gives you a chance to read your story in type. But every change that is made, no matter how small, will cost money. Anything that is put in or taken out means that one slug and sometimes more must be taken out of the galleys, discarded, and replaced by a new slug.

Everyone checks the galley proofs. You do. The editor does. The copy editor reads and double checks as she transfers the corrections to the master set. Before the master set goes back to the production man's desk, the designer notes the changes that have been made.

At about this same time, the designer also receives proofs of the illustrations for your book. While the type was being set and checked and changed, the illustrations were also taking shape.

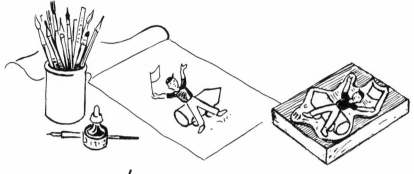

4 / Pictures in Metal

"Fourteen pages of black-and-white drawings — well, with luck I might be able to finish them in four weeks, but I'd rather say six in case I hit a snag." This is what the artist told your editor the day he dropped in to see her, soon after you had been there.

Having just finished a set of drawings for a magazine, he was free to do the illustrations for your book. And he was pleased with what the editor told him of the story. It sounded like a job that would be fun to do. As they talked, the artist noted down the page size and the amount of space the designer had allowed for illustrations. He knew he could divide the space as he liked as long as the pictures were well spread through the story. Finally, putting the carbon copy of your manuscript into his portfolio, he headed for home.

This artist has his studio at home. It is a large back room on the second floor, filled with worktables and cabinets, bookshelves and a filing case. Near one window is the drawing board, which has an edge well dented by thumbtacks and marked with telltale swipes of black ink. Here is where the drawings will take shape after the artist has read your story and done some planning.

The copy editor and the artist may be reading your story at the same time, but they will be reading it in quite different ways.

The copy editor is slowly, carefully going over your manuscript with an eye to its accuracy and style. The artist, on the other hand, is skimming through the carbon copy, watching only for the pictures your words form in his mind. He is alert to your description of the characters — how they would look and move and sound. He is also watching for the especially exciting and important moments in the story and scribbling down fast notes so that later he can select the scenes he wants to illustrate.

The word "illustration" comes from the Latin words that mean "to throw light on," that is, to make something clearer. An illustration is therefore a special kind of drawing. It must not only be interesting in itself, but it must also add something to a reader's understanding or enjoyment of the story.

One thing that the artist feels would add to your readers' fun is at least one good picture of your hero's invention, showing all the details. It will take research to get just the right kind of detail for such a device. Some of this he does in the file of newspaper and magazine pictures that he has saved over a period of years. Other ideas he picks up on a trip to the public library and the industrial museum. And a great variety of suggestions come from a group of the neighborhood boys who are fixing up an old car.

With this supply of ideas, the artist settles down to planning his compositions. Composition is one of those flexible words that can mean different things to different people. The typesetter uses this word to mean setting the type for your book. He considers his composition good if it is clean and evenly spaced. The artist uses the same word to mean the way in which he places the people and objects within the space of his picture. To him, good composition means an interesting balance of shapes and lines.

These drawings may take shape quickly or there may be a wastebasket full of crumpled, discarded sketches. Your artist prefers to start with these rough pencil sketches. Another might

begin right away on the final drawings and redo them if it is necessary. No two artists will work in exactly the same way, nor will they necessarily use the same tools.

In the short, sturdy chest that stands near the drawing board, your artist keeps some of his wide variety of tools. Here are the sleek, pointed brushes for water color and the square bristly ones for oil paint. There is a collection of pen points in all sizes and shapes, a row of green art pencils, round greasy crayons, v-shaped wood gougers, thin scalpel-like knives, as well as bottles and tubes of paints and inks. All these and many more things are at hand, not to mention a great assortment of different kinds and colors of paper. But only two or three of these materials will be used for any one job. Which he chooses depend on how the artist decides to do the illustrations.

The editor has asked the artist to do line drawings for your book. He has decided to do these line drawings in pen and ink. Therefore, the black India ink is uncorked, two brushes inspected, and a new dartlike point put into the penholder. Some heavy white paper is cut to size, and the artist is ready to begin. A tube of white paint and a brush are kept close by to touch up mistakes and cover any smudges.

Quick, sure pen lines — now thin, now heavy — and the shapes of people and objects appear on the paper. More lines, short and close, and spots of solid black are put in as the artist adds texture and shading to the drawing.

As he works, the artist keeps all the lines and spots solidly black and clean. Nowhere does he let them fade off into gray. By doing this, he is making a line drawing. For another kind of book he might have been asked to do halftone drawings. Then the artist could have used not only solid black but all the shades, or tones, of gray as well. A halftone drawing is one that has both the full solid color and lighter or "half" tones of the color. Though the artist is not using halftones for the drawings inside your book, he will use them on the jacket.

This distinction between line and halftone drawings is important because each is reproduced differently. The finished drawings that the artist delivers to your editor must, like your manuscript, be turned into something that can be printed. The new form for the drawings must look as much like the original

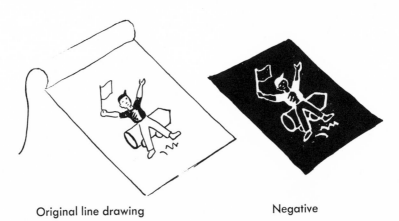

Original line drawing   Negative

drawings as possible. The drawings must therefore be made again, that is, reproduced, in metal.

The first printed pictures were made with wooden blocks, and often it was the artist himself who carved his pictures on the blocks. Much of this early printing of pictures was done in France, where the word for carve was *grave*. Later these pictures were made on metal. Metal can be cut into, or engraved, with special tools. It can also be eaten into, or etched, with acid. In either case, it is generally the white areas of the picture that are cut or eaten away. The lines and spots of the picture are then higher than the rest of the piece of metal, so that only they will hold the ink and print. Most of the illustrations that now appear in books are reproduced by a process that makes use of both etching and engraving, called photoengraving. Once the line drawings for your book have been checked to see that they follow the story accurately and that they are the right size, the manufacturing man sends them to one of the companies that does this work.

Walk into a photoengraving plant and your nose will immediately give you a clue as to the first step in this process. The air in the big room is filled with the pungent smell of hypo, a chemical used in processing photographic film. There are three giant

Photoengraving or "cut"   Printed illustration

cameras in the room, and in front of one of them is a large copy-board to which the drawings for your book are being fastened. On either side of the camera are carbon arc lights. When these are turned on, they will throw a brilliant light on the drawing while sputtering and giving off an eerie smoke.

The cameraman focuses his camera, exposes the film, and then takes it into one of the red-lit developing rooms. Here he will develop the negatives. These will then join a fluttering line of shiny black negatives, hanging up to dry at the far end of the room. A negative is the exact opposite of the drawing. Where the drawing is white, the negative is opaque and black. Where there are black lines and spots on the drawing, the negative is transparent.

Hanging near your negatives are others that have spots on them that look gray. If you look again, and this time with the aid of a magnifying glass, you will find that what looks gray is really a pattern of tiny black dots of various sizes. There is no real gray anywhere. These are the negatives made from halftone drawings, not from line drawings such as those for your book.

Back at one of the cameras you can see how this dotted negative was made. On the copyboard is a photograph or a drawing done in black and gray. This time before focusing the camera and exposing the film, the cameraman slides a special piece of lined glass into the camera. This is what he calls a screen. In some ways it is like a wire window screen, only very much finer. Just as a wire screen divides what you see outside the window into hundreds of little squares, the halftone screen divides what the camera "sees" into tiny squares. These squares are so small that they look like dots.

When you look directly at the sun through a window screen, the wires will seem to disappear and the squares will seem to grow bigger. Look at a dark object and the wires seem thicker and the squares smaller. This is a trick that light plays on your eye. The camera "sees" much as your eye does and records what it sees on the film. It records big dots where the picture on the copyboard is white, smaller ones where it is gray. As the shades of gray become darker, the dots become smaller until they are tiny where there is black in the picture. When you see the printed picture, your eyes will translate these dots back into the different shades of gray. But despite what you think you see, there is

nothing on the page but black and white dots of different sizes.

Once the negatives for your line drawings are dry, they are fastened to pieces of heavy glass called flats. It will take two flats to hold all the drawings for your book. These are then taken into the next room. This room also has several of the arc lamps that give off such strong light, and there is a large framed surface that looks like the copyboard for the camera. But this time there is no camera or film.

One of the men in charge studies your two flats for a minute and then goes to a rack holding flat sheets of zinc and copper. These sheets are called plates, and it is a zinc plate that the man pulls out to begin your job. The copper would be used for halftones or for line cuts with many fine lines.

At the far side of the room, the zinc plate is laid into a large round tub. Here the room is quite dark, for onto the plate is being poured a coating sensitive to light. Then the plate is lifted over and placed on the surface under the frame. The glass flat with its negatives is also put under the frame directly on top of the plate. Closed, the frame holds these two tightly together.

The bright arc lights are turned on. Now the negatives act like a stencil. Where they are transparent, the bright light goes through and strikes the coating on the plate. Such strong light hardens the sensitive coating in these spots. Where the negative is black and opaque, no light can get through to the coating and so those spots remain soft.

In a few minutes the plate is pulled out of the frame and dunked into a blue alcohol bath. The alcohol washes away whatever coating is still soft. A blue dye in the alcohol stains the lines and spots of hardened coating that remain. This shows up the picture in bright blue so that when the plate comes out of the bath, the man can easily check it.

The coating has to be hard and clean so that it can resist a powerful acid. The acid will be used to eat away the uncoated metal, the part of the picture that is to be white. This will leave the lines and spots of the drawing raised and ready to print.

Watch out for Dragon's Blood! This is the red powder that has settled in a faint haze over everything in another part of the room. The etcher is brushing it onto a plate, for this powder, when heated and fused, also resists acid. It is used between bites of the acid to protect the sides of the raised lines. Each dip into the acid bath is called a bite, and your plates will probably go in four times. Since the acid eats away the metal very quickly, none of these bites takes long. But they must be watched carefully so that just the right amount of metal is eaten away and in just the right places. When the last bite is finished, the plate is washed and goes to a routing machine. This machine cuts even more metal from any large spaces that are to be white. Now the plates are ready for a trial printing.

Proofs of the illustrations are printed on plate-sized pieces of paper and then compared with the original drawings. If a small line or spot needs to be taken out, one of the hand engravers does it. Very little can be added to the plates. When the proofs pass inspection, they are sent to the publisher.

Here again the proofs are checked against the original drawings. Should any more corrections be needed, they will be made and another set of proofs printed. When the proofs are finally okayed, the individual illustrations on the plate are separated and glued or nailed to wooden blocks. The plates on these blocks are now exactly as high as type, so that they can be easily fitted with the Linotype slugs.

The proper name for these "metal pictures" is photoengravings, but far more often you will hear them called cuts — either line cuts or halftone cuts. The photoengraver, finished with his part of the work, ships the line cuts to the printer. Type and line cuts — the words and the pictures for your book — are now ready to be combined.

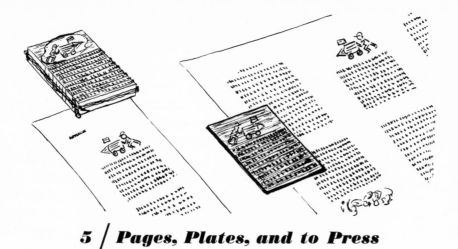

5 / Pages, Plates, and to Press

A set of galley proofs, the two sheets of illustration proofs, scissors, a jar of paste, and a book with blank pages — with these materials spread in front of him, the designer begins to make a dummy. The dummy is a cut-and-paste version of your book that shows just how the type and the illustrations are to be arranged on each page. If there were no illustrations, a dummy would probably not be necessary. Each page would then generally be made up with the same number of lines.

But when there are a number of illustrations, as in your book, the designer will probably have to do a little space juggling. Before he pastes down the pieces of galley and illustration proof, he may decide to move a few lines forward or back a page. By adding a little space here or taking it away there, he is working to make each page a well-designed unit.

When he is satisfied, the dummy will go to the composing room as a guide to the makeup man whose job it is to divide the long columns of slugs into page lengths, putting the line cuts in as he goes. With the dummy goes the master set of galley proofs. All the changes that you and the editor wanted have been marked on this master set, and these are the first things to be taken care of.

The changes go to the Linotype operator who swiftly sets the new slugs. Once these new slugs have been checked for accuracy, they are handed over to the makeup man who will put them in place.

On the long worktable in front of him are the first of the galley trays that hold the slugs for your book. The line cuts are also there — out of the newspaper wrappings in which they came from the photoengraver.

Deftly the makeup man begins to measure off the slugs. As he separates a group for a page, he slides in two additional slugs. One has the page number on it and goes in at the bottom. The other has either the book or chapter title and goes in at the top. This done, he pulls a length of string from a nearby ball and with several twists of his hand loops it tightly round and round the group of slugs. The loose end is skillfully tucked in, and this page is now held firm. None of the pieces will move.

There are finally 192 pages — some with only slugs, some with slugs and a line cut. These go to the proving press. Although they are still in the galley trays, the slugs are now divided into pages. The new proofs made from the type in these trays are therefore called page proofs.

These first go to the proofroom to be checked and then are sent to the publishing house with the galley proofs. They are checked by the designer, they are checked by the copy editor, and they are checked by you. Page proofs are checked and checked again, for once they are okayed, the slugs will be locked up. After this it is difficult to make changes.

Locking up type is done by a stoneman. This member of the composing room gets his name from the large square table at which he works. The smooth, even surface of this table is now made of steel, but for hundreds of years it was made of polished stone and so is still called the imposing stone. The stoneman's other equipment includes everything but a lock: a chase, furniture, quoins (pronounced coins), a quoin key, a planer, and a mallet. Only the mallet is what you might expect it to be from the name.

The chase is a heavy iron frame that is put around several pages of slugs—in your case, six placed side by side. Around and between the six groups go blocks of wood or metal called furniture. These touch the chase on all four sides. On two sides, the wedge-shaped metal pieces called quoins are put in near the edge. These quoins work in pairs. With the key they are made to overlap until they are absolutely tight, thus keeping the type and furniture from moving when the chase is lifted.

Before the quoins are given a final tightening, the stoneman moves a planer over the type. This smooth-bottomed piece of wood that looks something like a blackboard eraser protects the type as he taps with the mallet to be sure that no piece is standing higher than another. He then twists the quoins closed, and the first six pages of your book are locked up. A full chase like this one is referred to as a form.

Beyond the large rack where the chases are stored is the door to the foundry. This is the next stop for the forms. It is also the last stop for the slugs. In the foundry printing plates will be made. Once these are ready, the forms will be broken up. The line cuts will be stored and the slugs will go back to a melting pot for the Linotype machines.

For hundreds of years, printers put the forms directly on the press and printed from type. This is still done for special books, or when only a small number of copies are to be printed. In that case a larger chase and a different arrangement of the pages would be used. Books such as yours, however, are almost always printed from plates. A plate is an exact copy of the form except that instead of being made up of many slugs and line cuts, it is a single piece.

Until a few years ago, most plates were made of metal. Many still are, but now plastic and rubber are widely used.

The plates for your book will be made of plastic — a sturdy black opaque kind that comes to the foundry as a fine powder. Entering the foundry, you will feel a thin film of this gritty powder under your feet. But what you will feel even more is the heat that is coming from a large machine in the center of this room. It takes both heat and pressure to make this kind of plate.

To prepare a form for plating, the platemaker must first warm it on a metal heating table. A piece of a thin, stiff purple material, also warmed, is then laid on top of it, and the two are slid under pressure. If you get close enough to see the pressure gauge, you will find that the needle can go up as high as 200 tons. Push down that hard and the piece of material can't help but come out with every line, letter, and dot pressed sharply into it. This makes a perfect reverse copy of the form that can now be used as a mold.

The platemaker takes this mold, fills and covers it with the black plastic powder, and slides it back into the machine to be pressed and cooked. The plastic melts under the heat, filling in even the smallest turns and corners of the letters. When it cools, it becomes one solid piece of plastic. Pull this plastic plate from the mold and you have an exact copy of the six-page form.

The six pages in black plastic say the same thing as the gray slugs and line cuts. But hold the plastic in one hand and the heavy form in the other and you will quickly understand one of the advantages of plastic plates. They are far lighter than any metal would be. The six pages are cut apart and stacked on a hand truck. When all the plates for your book are ready, they will be wheeled down the hall and into the pressroom.

Metal plates made by a similar heat and pressure process are called stereotypes and are widely used in printing newspapers. Other metal plates, especially those used for printing books, are made by quite a different process that is called electrotyping. Electrotypes are copies made by means of electricity and chemicals.

In another part of the foundry you will see the blue-green chemical baths in which electrotyping takes place. First a mold of either wax or plastic is made from the type. After being sprayed with a silver solution so that electricity can travel through it, the mold is hung in one of the baths. A piece of copper is hung in the tub near it. Wires are attached and the electricity is turned on. As if by magic a thin copper shell begins to form on the mold. This is of course not magic but a chemical process called electrolysis.

When the copper shell is completed, it is separated from the mold and backed up with metal so that it becomes a firm, hard plate ready for printing.

Setting the type, photoengraving the illustrations, locking up the pages, and making the plates — these preparations have taken about three months. Now at last your book is ready to go "on press."

The pressroom is the largest room in the whole printing plant and it is also probably the noisiest. Unlike the rapid clattering of the Linotype machines, the presses roll out a steady, loud, thumping beat. You will hear it even before you reach the pressroom and probably feel a touch of excitement as it grows louder and louder. Through the swinging doors and you are at the heart of this beat. Here, attended by squat columns of white paper, stand two rows of large black presses.

Their size is impressive. But not all of the presses are large — though at first it may seem so. At the far end of the room are several smaller presses used for printing jackets and circulars. Nor are all the presses the same shape. However, the machines that you see here are alike in that they all do letterpress printing.

There are three important methods of printing, of which letterpress is the oldest. Letterpress can also be called relief printing because the letters and lines that will be inked and printed are raised. They stand in relief, higher than the rest of the plate.

A second method of printing is called intaglio printing. For this kind of printing the lines and letters are etched into the plate, and so are below the surface. When the plate is inked, the ink sinks down into the letters rather than being held up on top of them. Photographic books and the picture sections of newspapers are often printed by this method.

The third important method is surface printing. For this the letters are neither raised as in relief printing nor etched into the

Relief   INK   Intaglio

Surface

plate as in intaglio printing. Instead, with the aid of chemistry, they simply rest on the surface of the plate.

Many books, particularly picture books, are printed by this third method, in a process that is called offset-lithography. The pages of your book are to be printed by letterpress, but the jacket is printed by offset-lithography. As the jacket is made, you will get a clearer idea of surface printing. But that is done at a different printing plant. Here only letterpress printing is done.

Your plates are wheeled over to a large one-cylinder press by the window. Not long after they arrive, the pressman and his assistant are bending over the bed of the press, fastening them into position. The bed of the press is the large flat surface that will move back and forth under the heavy cylinder. Attached to one end of the bed is what looks like a metal honeycomb. The plates are fastened to this by small metal catches that grasp the narrow edge of the plate and then hook down through the network of holes.

Sixty-four plates are put into position for this first run of the press. But these are not the first sixty-four pages of your book. For one thing, if page one is in this group, page two cannot be. Since page two must print on the back of page one, it will be in another batch of sixty-four plates. This press can print only one side of the paper at a time. The first batch of plates will print on one side of the large sheets of paper, and the second batch will later print on the other side. "We call that second run 'backing up' the sheets," the foreman of the pressroom explains.

If there are to be sixty-four pages printed on one side of a sheet and sixty-four pages on the other — that takes care of 128 of your 192 pages. Sixty-four more pages are still needed. These will be printed on another stack of sheets, with thirty-two pages on one side and thirty-two on the other. In all, it will take four runs of the press to print your book. One-and-a-half large sheets of paper will be used for each copy of the book.

The foreman shows you the pattern in which the pressman is arranging the first sixty-four plates. If you are good at puzzles, make a large copy of this pattern that is on the opposite page. Now try to fold it into a book. If you can, you will be doing what the folding machine must later do to your sheets in the bindery. A few weeks ago, the foreman explains, the binder sent over this pattern for your book. Such a pattern is called an imposition, and because there is a great variety of possible impositions, the binder always specifies the one the printer should follow for a particular book.

On the pattern the foreman shows you, the plates seem to be touching each other. But as you watch the pressman, you will see that he is leaving carefully measured space between them. This space will make the margins on the pages.

Putting the plates in position is only part of the preparation. Now comes the make-ready. The press is inked and several trial sheets are run through. One of these is checked to see that the imposition is correct. Another is taken to where it can be held up to the light.

The pressman turns this sheet over. On its reverse side you can see the impression the type has made on the paper. As you watch the pressman begin circling and double circling certain areas with a soft black pencil, you will notice that in some spots the type has come through more heavily than in others.

"To help correct this uneven impression," says the foreman, "we'll make an overlay. On the back of this sheet, following his marks, the pressman will build up the places that are coming

Cut along the heavy lines.

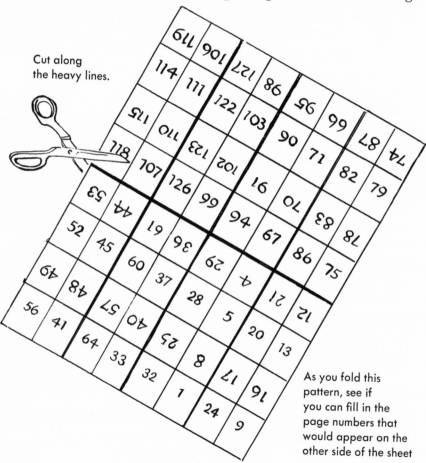

As you fold this pattern, see if you can fill in the page numbers that would appear on the other side of the sheet

through too lightly and thin the places that are very heavy. When this overlay sheet is fastened around the cylinder and more sheets are printed, it will increase or decrease the pressure in those spots just enough to make the impression even."

The foreman takes you over to a table where the assistant pressman is beginning the overlay. "Cutting paper dolls" is what he calls it. With a glob of paste on the back of his hand, a razor-sharp knife, and some pieces of tissue-thin paper, he is rapidly cutting out copies of the odd-shaped circles and pasting them in places on the back of the sheet. Where the pressman has drawn a circle within a circle, the assistant cuts and pastes a double and sometimes a triple layer of thin paper. Where a spot is marked "S," he scrapes it thin, and where a spot is marked "X," he cuts it out altogether.

This overlay sheet with its patches and occasional holes is now taken back to the press and added to the packing that is fastened around the cylinder. The real surface of this cylinder is metal, but you will never see it, for there are layers and layers of paper packing over it. This packing is held on at a spot where there is a gap in the cylinder's round, smooth surface. Here, too, is the row of grippers that will hold the incoming sheets of paper as they go around and down against the plates to be printed. It is the cylinder's double job both to hold the paper and also to press it as it comes on the plates.

Another set of trial sheets is run. The foreman and the pressman go over these carefully. "It's still running light on the corner; otherwise it looks pretty good." A few more adjustments are made; another trial sheet is run and, after being inspected, is okayed. The make-ready for this first run is finished.

A man who is called the loader lifts an armful of paper from the skid and climbs up to the feeding platform. This platform is just over the plates. Here he sets the sheets in line with an automatic device that will feed one sheet at a time onto the cylinder, evenly, smoothly, and at just the right moment.

While the loader is setting up the sheets on the feeder, the pressman is at the other end of the press checking the ink fountain. The fountain is actually a trough that stretches along one end of the press and holds the thick, shiny printer's ink. This ink comes in cans, and as it is dipped into the fountain, you will see that it has something of the consistency of house paint. There are many different kinds as well as colors of ink, for different methods of printing and different kinds of paper require special inks.

Watch the press when it is running slowly and you will notice, as the bed moves back and forth, that it has two parts. One end has the honeycomb with the plates. The other end has a smooth surface glossed with ink. This is called the ink table. Over it moves a series of rollers. One of these picks up ink from the fountain. The rest spread the ink so that the final two rollers will give just the right coating to the plates as they slide forward.

The preparations are complete. The pressman pushes the starter button, and the press rumbles into action. In a few minutes it has

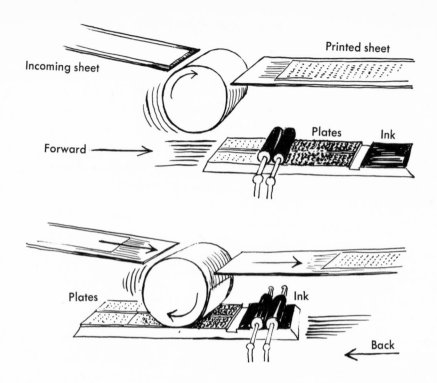

Incoming sheet

Printed sheet

Forward

Plates

Ink

Plates

Ink

Back

picked up speed and the run has begun in earnest. One by one the sheets are fed onto the cylinder, disappear for a second, and reappear at the top, wet with ink. The cylinder grippers let go, and another set of metal fingers seizes the sheet and delivers it to a platform at the far end. As each sheet goes along this delivery, you will catch a glimpse of flame. This draws off static electricity, which would keep the sheets from lying flat.

No sooner has a printed sheet settled on this delivery platform than another is right behind it, and then another and another. Automatically the platform lowers as the stack of finished sheets rises. The press is now going fast enough so that it is hard to spot the plates, but you can see the heavy bed moving in its rhythm, forward and back, forward and back. Moving forward, the plates go under the ink rollers; moving back, they have the paper pressed against them. As the bed goes forward, the cylinder raises a fraction of an inch. As the bed comes back, the cylinder has picked up paper and lowers again, going round against the plates. You will sense all this movement, but you would get a little dizzy if you tried to follow it at the speed the press is going.

The pressman has little to do now but watch, pulling out a finished sheet every so often to be sure the printing is coming out

clean and strong. Once they are going, presses are quite independent. But they are also very sensitive, and a slur here or a wrinkle there can quickly create a bad spot in the printing. A serious fault must be corrected in a hurry or dozens of sheets will show it.

There are to be eight thousand copies of your book, so eight thousand sheets, plus a small surplus, are printed in this first run. If there are no problems, it should be finished in about seven hours. The press is braked to a stop, and now one-third of your book is done.

As soon as these plates and the press have been cleaned, they are replaced by the second group of plates. Positioning the plates for this second run is easier. Since they must back up the first batch, they will line up in the same way. Make-ready, however, is still needed. It will probably be the next day before the second run begins. Once this second run is completed, this first stack of sheets is finished. They will be put aside to wait for the other batch.

All four runs will be finished in about three days. Your book is printed. The pictures and words are on paper, but at this stage in order to read it, one page after another, you would have to be an acrobat. These unwieldy sheets of pages are in need of folding and cutting. For this they are piled onto two large wooden skids and shipped off to the bindery.

6 / Colors and Chemicals

Another part of your book has already been delivered to the bindery. This is the paper jacket that will eventually be wrapped around the cover. Although it will not be needed until the very end, the jacket is printed well in advance so that extra copies can be used as a preview of your book for booksellers and librarians.

The jacket makes a good preview because — as well as keeping dust off the cover, the original purpose of a jacket — it was designed to give a quick, appealing idea of what the book is about. Part of this is done in words and part by the picture. The flap of the jacket that folds inside the front cover carries what is called the blurb. These few paragraphs try to say enough about your book so that people can judge whether or not they would like to read it. Your editor wrote the first draft of this blurb, but it was read and revised several times before it was ready to go to the typesetter.

The picture is almost as important as the blurb, and in it the artist has tried to reflect the humor and fun of your story. The jacket is in color. At their first meeting your editor had told the artist, "What we would like is a three-color picture, using halftones. And, of course, we're counting on your doing the separations."

The choice of the colors was up to the artist. Later in his studio,

he began to experiment with different combinations. Since this was to be a halftone drawing, the artist could use not only the three colors themselves but also a variety of shades and mixtures of them. For one sketch he decided upon a blue, a red-orange, and black. By mixing the blue and the red-orange, he made various shades of brown. These he used along with various shades of gray, light blue, and softer shades of red-orange.

It was this sketch that the editor and the artist thought would make the best jacket. He, therefore, painted up a square of the solid blue and one of the red-orange, cleaned his brushes, and put the paints away. The final drawing would not be done in color, nor would it be done in one piece.

In place of the paints, the artist set out two bottles of black ink. One was the same India ink that he used for the illustrations; the other was a slightly stickier ink that is used on acetate, which is a stiff transparent plastic. All of the spots and lines, whether black, blue, or red-orange will be drawn in black ink.

Out of a large sheet of acetate, the artist cut two pieces the size

of the jacket. A third piece of the same size he had cut from his regular heavy white drawing paper. The drawing for each color will go on a separate piece. The drawing for the black goes on the heavy white paper, the drawing for the blue on one piece of acetate, and the drawing for the red-orange on the other. Spots where the blue and red-orange mix to make brown are drawn on both pieces of acetate. One color will then print over the other.

These three drawings are called the color separations. This is only one of several ways in which colors can be separated. But by one means or another it must always be done for any kind of color printing. This is because each color must print separately. Though colors may sometimes be printed quickly one right after another, they are never printed together at exactly the same time. Therefore, each color must have its own printing plate, and for making these plates the colors in the picture must be separated.

Your artist makes his finished drawing in the form of three separations. This is not too difficult when you've had practice and when the colors are limited. But when the colors are not limited, as in a full-color oil painting, the separations are usually done photographically.

No matter how many colors there are in such a painting, the photographer can separate them into four basic colors. By this four-color process he can divide even the most complicated picture into yellow, red, blue, and black.

To do this, he photographs the painting four times, each time slipping a different filter into the camera. Each filter lets only one group of colors go through it to the film. An orange filter will let only the blues through, a green filter only the reds, and a violet filter only the yellows. A special combination of these will let just the black through. Thus he gets four "separation negatives."

He photographs each of these negatives, putting a halftone screen into the camera. The screen makes the pattern of dots that will give all the tones and shades. Again your eyes will be fooled by these fine dots, for when the picture is printed, you will not see the four colors of the printer's ink but the full array of shades and tones that were in the original painting. To uncover this trick, you need only take a strong magnifying glass to the printed picture and it will suddenly turn back into a pattern of overlapping red, yellow, blue, and black dots.

The dots overlap, but they are never on top of one another. This is intentional, for the trick would not work as well if your eye did not see part of each dot. However, when you look at a picture without a magnifying glass and the colors look as if they have slipped — the red for the mouth is not where the lips are drawn or a brown shoe has an orange outline on one side and a blue one on the other — that is not intentional! That is a mistake caused by bad register.

Proper register is when everything prints exactly where it is supposed to. It is important in all printing but especially in color printing. To aid the printer in this, your artist made register marks on all his separations. The first drawing that the artist did for your jacket was the black one. This acted as a key drawing. In each of the four margins, he marked a small neat cross. Then he put the first piece of acetate over this drawing and taped it securely in place. Once he was sure that it would not move, he traced the four crosses in the margins and started the drawing that would print in blue. Having finished the blue drawing, he taped the other piece of acetate over these two drawings and again traced the four crosses before beginning the drawing for the red-orange.

These four crosses are called the register marks. With these the separations can always be reassembled just as they were done. When the crosses fit over each other exactly, the spots of color will fit together.

Once the separations are finished, the artist mails them to the editor, enclosing with them his original sketch and the two color samples. The sketch shows where he has left space for the title and your name. These the designer has set in type along with the blurb about your book.

As soon as there is a perfect proof of this type, the designer returns it to the composing room marked, "O.K. Please pull repro proof." Reproduction proof is the full name for this final copy, and when it comes in, everyone handles it with special care. Unlike galley or page proof, reproduction proof is not used for checking or correcting type. It is to be photographed and so is printed crisp and black on a good grade of white paper.

The slugs from which the repro proof was printed will go back to the lead pot. No plate has been made from this type because raised letters are not needed as they were for letterpress printing. The repro proof and the separations will be handled in the same way, so together they are put into an envelope and sent off to a printer who specializes in offset-lithography.

The double name, offset-lithography, is a clue to the two important differences between this kind of printing and letterpress. The first word, "offset," indicates that the printing plate never touches the paper. The second word, "lithography," indicates that this is surface printing and the plate is practically smooth. Witchcraft! That is what early printers such as Gutenberg would have said to the idea of printing with a smooth plate that doesn't touch the paper. What, for instance, could possibly hold the ink in the shape of letters and lines?

What does hold the ink in these shapes is exactly the same thing that makes water slip off a duck's back — the chemical principle that oil and water don't mix. The duck has a natural coating of oil on his feathers that keeps the water off and so lets him float. Take this oil off and he sinks!

On the other hand, take water away from the offset-lithographer and he can't print. The lines and letters on the smooth offset plate have a thin oily surface. When water is put on this plate, it slips off these greasy letters and lines and dampens only the surface around them. When the printer then puts a greasy printing ink on the plate, it sticks to the letters but not the damp background.

This kind of plate is made by photography and light, so that some of the equipment in the offset platemaking department will remind you of the photoengraver's plant. The first stop for the repro proof and the separations is the camera room. This will look familiar, for the large camera and its copyboard and the bright sputtering arc lights are all like those you've seen before.

One after another the cameraman photographs the three separations. For each he uses a fine halftone screen. Then he takes out the screen and makes a fourth shot — this time of the repro proof. Photographing the type without a screen will make it sharper, since it will not be broken up into the tiny halftone dots. After the negatives are developed, this fourth one will be fastened, or stripped as it is called, to the negative of the black drawing.

The next room, where the stripping-up is done, has the colors of Halloween — black negatives, sheets of yellow-orange paper, stacks of yellow boxes, rolls of orange tape, and jars of red-brown paint. The negatives are to be stripped into the sheets of yellow-orange layout paper, using the orange tape.

First, however, your negatives are gone over by the retouch man. A soft light shines up through the frosted-glass table where he works. By putting a negative on this light table, he can check even the smallest dot or scratch. Next to the negative he has the original drawing. If a line or a dot is missing from the negative, he can scratch it in with a long sharp needle. More often flecks of light come through where they were not intended. These are covered with touches of red opaque, a pasty paint that dries to a red-brown color.

Once the negatives are stripped up, the three yellow-orange sheets to which they are taped are carried across the hall and slipped into a rack marked "Ready for Plating." Next to this rack is another one with sheets the same size but stiffer and less colorful. These are the thin gray sheets of metal that will be used for the printing plates. Some are zinc and others are aluminum.

As the platemaker pulls a plate out of the rack, it gives the bright bending sound of a cookie sheet, and you can see that one side is a dull whitish color and the other is slick and shiny.

"This shiny bottom side is the way the metal looks before it has been given its tooth — that is, before its been roughed up. Here, run your finger over the top. The tooth is so slight, you can't feel it, but it gives the surface ridges and valleys — otherwise we couldn't make a good plate."

As he tells you this, the platemaker is cleaning the plate first with a brush-and-water scrubbing and then with a mild acid solution. He lets it drip a minute and then lifts it over into a round, shallow tank called the whirler. The whirler's cover is up, and you can feel the heat from rods running across it. Looking down inside, you can see the platform on which the plate will spin. The plate is given a few spins to be sure it is completely dry. Then, as it continues to spin, the platemaker pours a slow thin column of brilliant yellow-green liquid onto it. As the plate goes round, this liquid spreads out in a growing circle of color until the whole plate has an even smooth coating. This liquid is made up of several chemicals, but it is called albumin because the most important ingredient in it is the white of eggs!

If you have ever tried to wash dried egg white out of a cup, you know that albumin is stubborn stuff. Combine this stubbornness with a chemical that is light sensitive, trap the combination in thousands of tiny valleys, harden it with a strong light, and you will have a coating that is on for good.

This is what will happen to the plate. In the whirler, the tooth on the plate traps and holds the light-sensitive coating. As the heat from the rods dries it, the coating becomes a pale yellow. The platemaker then quickly lifts the plate out of the whirler and onto a large vacuum table. The layout sheet with the first of your negatives is put on top of it. Down comes the glass top, pressing the two together. The whole of the plate is covered. Light cannot touch it except through the transparent lines and dots of the negative. With a sucking hum a pump draws out any air. Then the top of this table is tipped to face an arc light. The bright light is turned on and a timer is set.

In a few minutes the albumin will become hard wherever the light hits it. When the bell rings, the frame is opened and the bright yellow layout sheet laid aside. You will have to look closely to see the hardened lines and dots, just faintly yellower than the rest of the plate.

The plate is lifted over onto a black-splotched table where it will get another coating — this time of a smooth black developing ink.

Now back to the sink where the plate soaks in water for a minute or two. Standing over it, you can see the shapes and letters slowly appear, as tiny black flakes float to the surface. What begins to happen here, and what finishes very dramatically as the man swabs the plate, is that the albumin coating not touched by the light is dissolving and floating off with the layer of ink that was on it. The albumin that had been hardened by the light sticks in the valleys and holds tight to the ink on top of it. The blackened lines and dots look exactly as they will on the final printed sheet.

A last bath is applied with a large paint brush. This is frothy blue-green acid that will clean the plate's "teeth" wherever there is no hardened albumin. More water, a quick drying in front of a large fan, and the plate is finished. Before it is set aside, the plate will get a temporary coating of gum arabic to protect it until it reaches the press.

Pass your fingers over the plate now. Unless they are extraordinarily sensitive, you will feel no more than you did before. The hardened albumin is so slightly raised that the plate still feels smooth to the touch.

The plate for the black drawing is done. The platemaker pulls out a second piece of metal and begins the same process over again, this time using the negative for your red-orange drawing. Another plate is made for the blue, and within about an hour and

a half all three plates are finished and ready to go to the pressroom.

Not only is an offset plate light enough to carry, but it is also very flexible and can curve smoothly without bending or cracking. The plate must do this when it reaches the press. On the offset press, the plate does not rest on the bed of the press but is clamped around a large cylinder.

Cylinders and rollers — offset presses have a great number of them as you will notice when you follow the foreman through this pressroom. Though your jacket will be printed on a small press, the foreman first takes you over to one of his large ones.

This large press is being set up to run a picture book. As you watch the pressman clamp a plate into place, you will spot the plate cylinder as being about halfway up the press. Above it are rollers of all sizes. Below it, there are two other large cylinders that the foreman points out.

"This nearest one, which will touch the plate cylinder when the press is going, is the blanket cylinder. The rubber blanket around

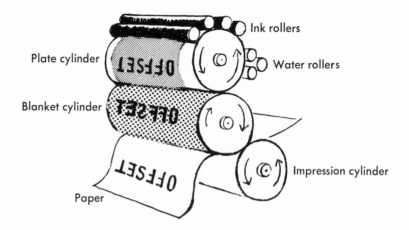

Plate cylinder — Ink rollers — Water rollers

Blanket cylinder

Impression cylinder

Paper

the cylinder is, you might say, a clue to why we call this offset printing. You'll see exactly why when the press is running."

Slightly below and to one side of the blanket cylinder you can just catch sight of the impression cylinder. The grippers on this third cylinder will take hold of each incoming sheet of paper and carry it around into contact with the rubber blanket. Out of sight below this impression cylinder is a delivery unit that will take the printed sheet as the grippers release it.

"Your jacket is going to be printed on the press over there. You can see by the ink rollers that the pressman's already got the red-orange on for the first run."

Having put on the first plate for your jacket, checked the rubber blanket, and loaded paper on the feeder, the pressman is now running proof sheets to check the color. While the press is going fairly slowly, as it is now, walk around it, keeping your eye on the plate cylinder. This is what you'll see. As the plate comes up and around, it first passes against two soft, damp water rollers. These moisten the non-printing parts of the plate. Immediately afterwards the plate passes against four of the ink rollers. As you can tell from the red-orange ink on them, there are many other ink rollers above these four. This assortment of rollers is spreading the ink being fed down from a long ink fountain so that the bottom four rollers will have the proper coating to pass onto the plate.

Dampened and inked, the plate disappears as the cylinder carries it down to print. But instead of now printing on paper, the plate rolls the ink onto the rubber blanket. The blanket cylinder is at the same time turning toward the impression cylinder. Here the blanket meets the paper. As the rubber blanket turns against the paper, it transfers, or offsets, the wet ink onto the paper. The sheet is printed. It now moves onto the delivery unit as the impression cylinder turns to pick up another. For every sheet of paper that is printed, the plate cylinder, the blanket cylinder, and the impression cylinder will each go around once.

A few sheets go through, and then the press is stopped as the

pressman and the foreman check them against the artist's color sample. Some adjustments, more proof sheets, and finally the color is okayed. The press is started up again, and this time it is allowed to reach cruising speed. The first run for your jacket is under way, as the press adds its steady rolling sound to the general roar of the pressroom. You can't ask many questions now, because of the noise. But as you watch, you will catch a flash of the plate as it takes the red ink down to the blanket and a second later reappears to get more water and then more ink. One by one the grippers of the delivery unit bring out sheets covered with red-orange lines and spots. They look like a senseless pattern, and it is hard to believe that by printing another color on top of that and then still another, they will actually turn into jackets. But they will!

"The blue will go on press this afternoon and the black tomorrow morning," explains the foreman as he shows you back to the office. By tomorrow afternoon there will be ten thousand finished copies of your jacket. These will then be ready to be shipped to the bindery.

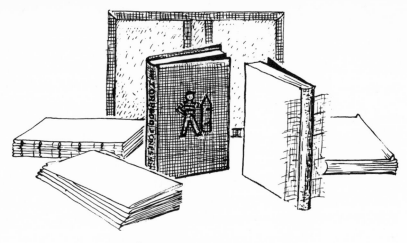

7 / Into the Covers

A man in the bindery office is talking to your production man over the phone. "The sheets arrived today, and according to our schedule they should go on the folder late tomorrow — or the next day. You'll have bound books in three weeks for sure."

As he talks, he runs his eyes down a list of specifications. Most of these words and figures will make no sense to you, but to this man they tell exactly what your book is going to look like and, more important, how it is going to be held together.

Almost all of a book's strength is in its spine, or back edge. Like your own backbone, little of this shows from the outside. In some books, however, you get a glimpse of what is under the cloth by looking down the spine from above. This way, you may be able to see that against the inside of the cloth is a layer of heavy gray paper and down the back of the pages themselves runs a strip of wrinkly tan paper. Under this tan lining is a strip of loosely woven cloth and, under that, a network of sewing threads. But both of these layers are completely hidden by the paper.

Another thing that you will see clearly by looking down the spine is that the pages are not on separate leaves each fastened at the back. Instead they are folded together in sections, which are called signatures. This name comes from tiny signs that were put on the first page of each section so that the sections would be gathered and bound in the right order. The signatures in English books still carry these tiny signs, but those in American books seldom if ever have them. Marks along the back fold are used instead.

In theory, a signature could have as few as four pages — one piece of paper folded to make two leaves. But in actual practice, they usually have eight or a multiple of eight pages. On the specifications for your book, you will see after the word "Signatures" these figures: 6/32's. This means that your book will have six signatures, each with thirty-two pages in it.

There are two kinds of folding machines and different sizes of each. Every one of these machines can fold several different patterns. This is why there are many patterns, or impositions, for arranging plates on the press. If folding the first sheet of your book still puzzles you, the bindery foreman can show you how it is done

55	42	63	34	31	2	23	10
50	47	58	39	26	7	18	15
51	46	59	38	27	6	19	14
54	43	62	35	30	3	22	11

1. This is half the sheet

2. Fold 54 up to 55

This diagram
shows how the tape and knife machine does step 2

by folding an imposition card similar to the one sent as a guide to your printer.

The first step was cutting the pattern in half. For this particular machine, all of your sheets will be cut in half before they are run through. As you follow the foreman into the plant itself, you will pass a large mechanical knife where this might have been done.

Turning the corner, you will see the row of folding machines. To get to these, you must make your way through rows of skids, stacked with paper. Some of these skids hold piles of flat printed sheets. Others have bundles of folded pages. From here on, all through the bindery, you will pass such paper-laden skids, standing like stout hedges around and between the different machines.

Your sheets are passed into the folding machine by a large->-shaped feeder at one end. The man who is loading it straightens the sheets to a guide so that they slide smoothly around and onto the bed of moving tapes.

This type of folder is called a tape and knife machine because

3. Make a second fold bringing 52 up to 53

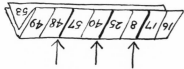

4. Cut along these three lines and turn the sections over

5. Fold 48 and 49 together, 40 and 51, 5 and 25, 16 and 17

6. Then you have this. Turn two to the left and two to the right

7. Move them together this way and you have the first two signatures of your book.

the tapes now carry the sheet until it is over two rollers and under a long knife. This knife has a dull edge, since it is not meant for cutting. The knife comes down and pushes the middle of the sheet between the rollers. As the sheet continues down through, this makes the first fold. Another set of rollers and a knife are waiting below to make a second fold. And for each following fold there is such a set. Some of these knives have small teeth along their edges that make tiny holes in the fold. These holes let trapped air escape so that the fold can be flat and smooth. All the knives that make the permanent back folds have dull edges. What cutting is needed is done by sharp round blades, the first of which you can see set between the tapes.

Actually, though you can hear the folding going on, there is little of it that you can see. At one end, large flat sheets, one by one, feed in and fold down under the knife. At the other, two rows of newly folded pages inch out along separate troughs. One holds copies of your first signature. The other holds copies of your second.

Every so often a man picks up an armload of signatures from one of these troughs and lines them up in a viselike bundler. A cardboard is slipped in at either end and pressure is applied. The line of signatures suddenly shrinks as the air between the pages is squeezed out. This is only the first of three times that your book will be squeezed to keep it firm and compact.

Cord is tied around each bundle as it is taken out of the bundler. Once it is stacked on a nearby skid, you can tell by the red numbers on the cardboard which of the six signatures is in the bundle. Those that hold the first and last signatures are taken over to the tipping machine. Here each of these signatures gets a line of paste along one side of its back fold, and to this is pressed a pair of endpapers. The endpapers are the heavier pages that are at the beginning and end of a book, sometimes with a special map or drawing on them. As the signatures come off the tipping machine, you can see that

the endpaper has two leaves. In the finished bound book, however, there will seem to be only one. The other leaf will be pasted to the cover, holding it in place.

From here, the first and last signatures move on to meet copies of the other four at the gathering machine. This machine is one of the bindery's most dramatic. If, with any of its arms, it picks up a faulty signature, there is a sudden and complete stop. A red marker is thrown up, and the machine does nothing more until the operator remedies the situation.

There is a marker for each of the signature-size bins that run along one side. Only six of these are needed for your book. Each will hold a pile of one of the signatures. In front of every bin is an angular metal arm with a two-fingered clamp that swings out and back, pulling out one signature at a time from the bottom of each pile, and dropping it on a moving conveyor belt. The last signature comes onto the belt first. Then as it moves past the next bins, the others are added in turn, until at the end of the machine all six are

in a pile. Each pile now has the pages for a complete book. It is picked up by a girl, quickly checked, and stacked on a skid.

Folded and gathered, the signatures are now ready to be fastened together. The skid full of books is moved into a room alive with the rapid sound of sewing machines. The first thing you'll notice about one of these machines is the line of giant spools of thread that stands along the top. For a book your size there will be five. For each spool there will be a needle. As you watch the woman threading these needles, you will see that each of them seems to have a "double" next to it. This "shadow" needle is actually a hook. The needle will take the thread down through the fold in the signature, and the hook will bring it back up, twisting and locking the stitch. Five needles, five hooks, and five threads will all be sewing at the same time.

The stitching begins. Opening the first signature at the middle, the sewer slips it over a feeder. This feeds it onto a metal arm. The signature will ride this arm up to the row of needles. As the first signature slips off and goes under the needles, the arm moves back to pick up the second, and then the third, fourth, fifth, and sixth. With barely a pause in the steady stitching rhythm, the first signature of the next book is over the arm and on its way through. Beyond the needles a solid white column of sewn books steadily grows longer and longer.

"All these books could come off the machine sewn together because the five threads are continuous," explains the foreman. "But the operator has a mechanical means of clipping the threads after every sixth signature and also a way of applying a quick line of paste along the inside back edge of the first and last signatures of each book just before those signatures go under the needles."

As your books are taken off the sewing machine, they are stacked in small piles, ready for the next step, which is called nipping. Nipping is a second squeezing, but this time it is only along the back edge, which has gotten fat in the folding and sewing.

Before leaving the sewing room, take a quick look at the different sewing machines farther down. The sewing you watched being done on your book is called Smyth sewing. There are two other important kinds of sewing used for books, side-sewing and saddle-sewing. Side-sewing is often used on school and library books that are going to get especially hard wear. Instead of each signature being sewed down the center of the fold, this machine sews all the

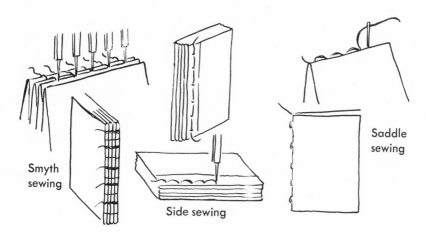

Smyth sewing

Side sewing

Saddle sewing

signatures at once along the side of the fold. There is only one stout needle that stitches a line from top to bottom.

The saddle-sewing machine also has just one needle, but it stitches through the center of the fold. This method is used when the book has only one signature, so you quite often see it in picture books.

There are some books, such as telephone directories and paperbacks, that never go through a sewing machine. They are given what is called Perfect Binding — a name that does not mean they are better bound than sewn books but only that there are no layers between the back of the pages and the cover. The pages are still folded as signatures, but, just before the cover is put on, the folded back edges are cut off. A strong glue is quickly applied, and this anchors each of the pages directly to the cover and to each other.

With sewing and nipping, the first part of the binding is done. These steps were the sheetwork. Now comes what is called the forwarding. The steps in this second part will build the spine of the book. The third and last part of binding, called the finishing, is the making of the cover and attaching it to the pages.

Glue, either yellow animal glue or a white synthetic kind, is important in the first step of the forwarding. As you enter the next room, you see a large pot of glue being kept warm near the machine that your books are now entering. This machine gives each book a good coating of glue along the spine. Enough is put on so that it will seep down a little way between the signatures. This will help to hold the signatures together. The glue is given time to dry thoroughly, and then the books are sent to the trimmer.

The trimmer, a giant three-knived cutter, will give your book a haircut. Up to this point the top, front, and bottom edges have had a shaggy, uneven look. A run through the trimmer and the pages come out with neat, clean edges.

Now comes the shaping of the spine. At present, both the spine

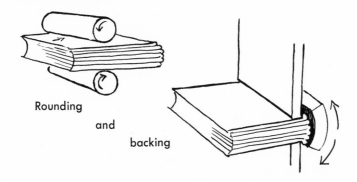

Rounding and backing

and the front edge of your book are straight and flat. If they re-
mained this way, the spine would be weak and the middle signatures would eventually push forward. There would also be a tend-
ency for the book to fall open always at the middle of the signature.
Therefore, in the next machine it is rounded and backed.

As the book goes into this machine, it is pressed through a pair
of rollers. These are the rounders, which, as they turn, pull the
signatures so that the front edge of the pages rounds in and the
spine curves out. A jaw next clamps the spine on each side, just
where the curve begins, and a heavy concave backing iron rocks
up and down on it. As the iron does this, it squashes and slightly
folds the back of each signature so that it bends sideways.

Backing the books in this way secures the signatures firmly in
place. It also makes joints at each side of the spine into which the
hinges will fit. Look at the covers on a finished book and you will
see that where they meet the spine there is a small dip. This is
called the hinge. Like a door hinge, this is what the cover swings
open and shut on.

Once rounded and backed, your books are ready for the lining
machine. Spine down, the books move into this machine to receive
several layers of strength. First, some flexible glue is rolled on, then
a wide strip of loosely woven cloth, more glue, and a strip of tan

paper, and then more rollers press all this tight. Out the other end comes a book ready for its cover.

On one side of the lining machine is a roll of the loosely woven white cloth, called crash, which looks very much like the gauze used in bandages. For each book, the cutter slices off a strip a little shorter than the length of the spine and passes it into the machine. The strip is two inches or so wider than the spine so that it can overlap on both sides. This will help the endpapers hold the cover when it is put on.

The wrinkly tan paper, which is called krinkle-kraft paper, feeds into the machine from another, narrower roll. This is cut into strips that are just as long and as wide as the spine. This paper holds the crash in place and helps keep the book from opening too sharply.

"All of these steps mean that your book can have a strong flexible spine unless the first reader opens the book abruptly, cracking and straining it," points out the foreman.

Your book will get just these two layers. Others might be given additional ones depending on the strength they needed. For decoration, some books will also be given a colored banding at the top of their lining, called the headband. With these layers the spine is complete and the forwarding is done. The books are moved over to the casing-in machine.

"What you call the cover, we call the case," the foreman says as you enter the casemaking room. "Casing-in is attaching the cover to the book, but that is one of the last steps of finishing the binding. The cases had first to be made. We did that several days ago so that they would be ready now. Your case was cloth over boards with ink stamping."

Light blue cloth is the part of your case that will be seen, but it is the two gray Binder's Boards underneath that will give the case its stiffness and protect the pages. Hundreds of years ago when books were few and very expensive, covers had boards that were actually pieces of wood. These treasured books had thick planks of oak covered with leather and decorated with precious stones. After the invention of printing, books became less and less expensive and the bindings became less and less elaborate. Some books, especially the beautiful hand-bound ones, are still covered in leather but no longer do they have wooden boards. The boards used now are made of fibres that are obtained from such things as straw, wastepaper, wood chips, and rope.

The light blue cloth for your cover came from the mill on a large roll and was stored for a while in what looks like a giant yardgoods section. On the shelves are rolls of cloth in every color and in several different qualities. The quality of the cloth depends on the kind of thread and how it was woven. Some, such as buckram, which is used on school books, has thick threads woven tightly together. Other kinds have looser weaves. The kind to be used for your book is not as tough or as expensive as buckram, but it still will take a good deal of wear.

The first step is to cut both the boards and the cloth to the proper sizes. The boards must be large enough to extend a fraction of an inch beyond the pages on the three open sides. The rectangle of cloth must be long and wide enough to turn over the edges of the boards. There must be just the right amount of room left for a strip of heavy gray paper where the spine will be and for the hinges on either side of it.

Onto the casemaking machine go all of these parts. The cloth picks up a coating of glue as it goes in and then settles on a platform, glue side up. Around swing red-tubed suction holders with two pieces of board and a strip of gray paper. They place these in position, and the cloth is then neatly turned in over the edges. As this case moves on to be pressed, another piece of cloth comes onto the platform for the next case.

This machine is a square solid one. Near it, is another kind of casemaking machine that looks quite different. On this long low machine, the cloth for the separate cases has not been cut but rolls onto the machine in one long piece. Only near the end are the cases slit apart. Your cases could have been made on this machine also.

Unless the cases are made with printed cloth or paper, their next step is the stamping machine. Here your cases will get the title put on their spines and a small decoration on the front cover. Stamping is much like printing except that there is more push to it. Lead type would not be strong enough to stand this push, so both the title and the decoration are made of brass. These pieces of brass are called the dies.

As each case is slid into the machine, these dies thump into it. For your cases the dies are inked in brown and leave the letters dark and clear against the light blue.

Nearby, cases are being stamped in real gold, and around the base of that machine lie great folds of metal foil. A long ribbon of this metal foil is being used instead of ink. The die is heated, and

as it comes down against the foil ribbon, it transfers gold in the shape of the design to the case, which is directly below. The used part of the ribbon moves on inch by inch and eventually folds onto the floor. It won't be thrown away, however, for there is still a thin layer of gold foil where the design was not taken off. This can be sold to be remade into new ribbon.

When all of your cases have been stamped, there will be some eight thousand of them stacked on several skids. As your pages begin going through the lining machine, these skids are moved over to one wing of the casing-in machine. There are three upright metal plates, or wings, that are slowly turning round in a circle.

Opening an unbound book near the middle, the operator slips it onto an empty wing. This wing turns a third of the way round and moves downward. When it comes up, it brings the book between two paste rollers. Just over the rollers waits a case, and as the wing brings the book up under it, the cover flops down against the paste-covered endpapers. The wing moves on, and another man lifts off the newly cased book. He pushes the book firmly into the case, sees that the corners are square, and then sets it aside on a table.

The book won't stay there long. The paste is wet, and there are no real hinges. If it were to dry this way, the book would be weak and sloppy. So your book now gets its third and final squeezing. The two men you see nearby are layering these newly finished books between pieces of brass-bound cherry wood. The brass is just slightly wider than the wood. As the men spread out a layer of six books, they let the spines hang beyond the edge so that the brass rim will press up to form one hinge. The other hinge will be pressed in by the brass on the piece of wood that will be put on next. When there is a fair-sized tower of books and wood, pressure is brought down on it. It sinks a few inches and iron bars are adjusted at the sides to hold it this way.

The next morning your books are released and sent to a row of women who have piles of the long unfolded jackets in front of them. Each of your eight thousand books will be picked up, quickly checked, and then jacketed by one of the women. The last stop is the shipping room where they are packed on skids and loaded into a truck for their trip to the publisher's warehouse.

These skids hold the first edition of your book. If in a year or so more copies are needed, a second edition will be printed and bound. But before that these eight thousand books must find their way to readers.

8 / *On Its Way*

One day, when you're not expecting anything special, a mail truck rolls up in front of your house. A package is brought to the door, and as you accept it, you see that it is marked BOOKS. This, you suddenly realize, is no ordinary package. This is the one you've been wanting to see for months! Unwrapping takes forever. Paper, cardboard, more paper, and then you spot the blue jacket and for the first time see finished copies of your book.

As the author, the publisher will send you ten copies altogether. Picking one up and turning the trim white pages, you find it hard to believe that this could really be your story. The words are yours, but what a far cry these books are from the manuscript you first sent the editor eight months ago. And what pleasant compactness after the unwieldy page proofs — the last you saw of your book, almost two months ago.

A letter from your editor also arrives. She is delighted with the way the book turned out and hopes that you are too. She is also writing to let you know the publication date. This will be in six weeks. Though the book is now finished, it is not officially published. These six weeks before publication give time for bookstores to receive their shipments and for copies to go to reviewers.

The review copies of your book are being sent out by one of the publicity assistants. "On that new children's book," she says, checking with your editor, "we're sending copies to all the newspapers and magazines that regularly list and review children's books, and though neither of the papers in the author's home town runs book reviews, we'll send copies with a special letter and a photograph in case they want to do a feature story." Other copies will go to large libraries that may order many copies and to the organizations that make up special state and national listings.

Publicity, promotion, and advertising are the three means a publishing house uses to let people know about new books. There are eight thousand copies of your book waiting to be purchased and read. Before this can happen, people must hear of your book and stores and libraries must order it. Along with your book, there are fifty other new adult and children's books that the trade department of your publisher is bringing out the same season.

The publicity, promotion, and advertising will be done differently for each book. They will be planned so that they reach as many people as possible, but most particularly those people who would be especially interested in buying that kind of book. Librarians who select the children's books for school and public libraries will, for example, want to know about your book. Eventually they will hear of it through reviews in magazines such as *The Booklist, Junior Libraries,* and *The Horn Book.* But that will be well after publication date. Before then, the promotion people reach most of them through the special catalog of new children's books that they send out. There may also be a circular or newsletter that they send from time to time.

For catalogs, circulars, and ads, special "copy" — sentences or paragraphs about your book — is written. Writing such copy is something like entering one of the contests that begins, "In a hundred words or less write . . ." In a short space, the copy writer must give something about the plot and characters, something about the special qualities of the book, and something about who might enjoy it most. These words must be chosen and put together in such an intriguing way that people will want to read all they have to say.

Still another way that the promotion people will let librarians know about your book is by exhibiting it at special conventions and meetings and by putting it in various traveling exhibits that move around the country. Even while the book was still being printed, the jacket was being displayed — at the annual American Booksellers Association convention and at the American Library Association convention. It is during this latter convention, at a gala dinner, that the Newbery and Caldecott Medals are awarded to two outstanding children's books chosen from among the twelve hundred or so published the previous year.

The selling of your book begins even before this. It began in May or early June. That was when the publishing house held its Fall Sales Conference. Your publishing house holds two conferences, one in May or early June to introduce and discuss the books to be published in the fall, and one in December to do the same for the books to be published during the coming spring.

There is excitement in the air on the morning that Sales Conference begins. From all the offices, people gather in the large conference room. Notes in hand, the editors congregate at the front of the room. Near your editor, the designer is checking through the jackets and sample pages he has brought in for her to show as she talks about each book.

The advertising manager is talking with the sales manager who will direct the meeting. On the table in front of them is a folder holding sketches for several large ads. Most of these are for adult books, but one of them might be the Children's Book Week ad in which your book will appear. These sketches have been made by an advertising agency, and several people from the agency have come over to attend the conference. When the sketches have been approved, the agency will put them in a finished form and send them to newspapers and magazines according to the advertising manager's plan.

As the salesmen come into the room, they exchange greetings and news of their spring selling trips that have just ended. For several of these eight men, sales conference is the only time they get into the office. It is the only time when all eight of them are together, and there is always plenty to talk about.

Finally the conversation dies down, people settle into their chairs, and the sales manager opens the meeting. This conference will begin with the presentation of the children's books. Your book is fourth on the list. Some people in the publishing house already know your book and have worked on it, but now it is to be officially introduced to everyone.

Your editor makes the introduction. She gives a snatch of the story, a feeling of its humor, and an idea of what makes this book different from others. There is a color proof of the jacket to show and some of the illustrations. Since it is a children's book, she will also suggest the age group that might enjoy your book most.

The sales manager then sums up the presentation of your book by saying, "This obviously should have a sound market through both bookstores and libraries. Let's try for a thirty-five hundred advance." By advance he means the number of books that will be ordered before publication day.

Your editor's introduction took barely seven minutes, but they are an important seven minutes in the life of your book. The salesmen, who are meeting your book for the first time, are the vital link between the publisher and the bookstore.

The conference lasts three days because there is much to be discussed. And then, with many handshakes and last-minute con-

versations, the salesmen are on their way, each to a different part of the country. In their bags are jackets of the new books, sample pages and illustrations, catalogs, and a large supply of the blue order forms with the titles listed on them.

Just as no two publishing houses are exactly alike, no two bookstores are either. Not only do they vary in size and shape, but more important they vary in the kinds of books they want and can sell. After a few calls, a salesman will know the kinds that interest a particular bookseller and also how many copies that bookseller should order. If he orders too few, he will run short. If he orders too many, he will eventually want to return some. Neither is good business, so the salesman tries to help him avoid both.

"Hello. Good to see you," calls the bookseller as your salesman enters. "Be with you in a second." He rings up a sale, wraps the book, and then sits down at his desk with the salesman.

"How were things in New York? Going to have any good books this fall? Say, seriously, I want to put in my children's book order earlier this year. We are going to help the PTA put on a book fair in November."

Turning through the jackets, the salesman briefly presents each of the new books. Your editor introduced your book in seven minutes; the salesman must now do it in three or four.

"Put me down for ten on that — we should sell that many before Christmas," says the bookseller. Next to your title on the blue order form, the salesman jots the number ten. Across from your title, in a column marked "List Price," is the price at which the bookseller must sell your book. But he will not pay that much to the publisher for it. He will get a discount of a certain per cent. The difference between what he pays for the book and what he sells it for allows him to cover his expenses and make some profit.

After ordering the new books, the bookseller will probably give the salesman a backlist order as well. These are books published last year and earlier that he wants to reorder. By next year your book will be on the backlist. It will stay on the backlist as long as enough people continue to buy it so that it can stay in print.

The blue order form is mailed back to the publishing house and ten copies of your book are sent to the bookstore in time for the publication date. With ordinary luck these ten copies will be sold by December, and the bookseller will send in another order for more copies to sell at Christmas time.

Soon after publication day, orders begin to arrive from libraries, and more copies of your book are shipped out to them. Most libraries, however, do not buy from most publishers directly but from wholesale companies, called jobbers, who handle the books of many different publishers.

Not long after a copy of your book arrives in a library, it is given a card and a card pocket, and sometimes a clear plastic cover over its jacket. Thus equipped, it is ready for service. The children's librarian files author, title and subject cards for it in the card catalog and finds a place for your book on a shelf.

The children's librarian is one of the best friends your book will have. You, the editor, the artist, the designer — all the people who have worked on your book — have tried to make it one that children will enjoy. But not everyone is going to enjoy it equally well. Some may not like it at all. Others, happily, will think it is wonderful. By knowing the books and talking with the children who come to her library, the librarian helps your book find its way to the readers who will enjoy it.

If it's your book that wins the praise, "That's the best book I've ever read," the librarian will remember. Long after this copy is old and battered and replaced by other copies, the librarian will be giving your book to new and enthusiastic readers. She will be completing this story that you began when you first sat down to write a book.

Index

655
F
FOSTER, JOANNA
   Pages, pictures, and print

F65-834

655
F
FOSTER, JOANNA
  Pages, pictures, and print

F65-834

DATE DUE	BORROWER'S NAME	3.27 ROOM NUMBER
JAN 3 '66	Denny Darl	116
MAR 4 '77	Bill Via	209

Index

655
F
FOSTER, JOANNA
 Pages, pictures, and print

F65-834

FAIRLESS HIGH SCHOOL

Navarre, Ohio